Original Title: How to Listen to your INTUITION
Copyright © 2023 Swan Charm Publishing
All rights reserved.

Editors: Jessica Elisabeth Luik
Autor: Swan Charm
ISBN 978-9916-660-66-9

How to Listen
to your INTUITION

Swan Charm

The Hidden Interpreter

Long ago, a foreign merchant, Elijah, known for his trade acumen, revealed his secret only to his successor, his son David. He introduced David to an imaginary persona, 'The Hidden Interpreter'. 'It's not another person,' the father clarified, seeing David's perplexed look. 'It's a part of me. When decisions seem complex, I listen to my interpreter.'

David, despite skepticism, decided to give it a go and was amazed. Conversations with clients, even in foreign tongues, were smoothly interpreted by this hidden interpreter in his father's way. The whirlpool of numbers, prices, and commodities seemed to align perfectly whenever this voice guided him.

David realized that his father had instilled in him a sharp instinct, an intuition that cut through chaos, confusion, and complexity. The unseen interpreter was actually a manifestation of his inherent wisdom. And so, the skillful merchant's legacy lived on, guided by their found wisdom.

The Mute Violinist's Melody

A long time ago in a bustling city, lived an ordinary boy named Leo, who had an extraordinary talent. Leo was a mute from birth, but he possessed a unique ability to play the violin. Every stroke of his bow, every subtle movement of his fingers, told stories that words could hardly express. Listening to Leo, one could hear whispering winds, rolling waves, and even the silent dance of stars in the cosmos.

Leo was usually ignored by the bustling crowd, for they were too entrapped in the 'now'. However, there were a few who would pause and immerse themselves in the symphony Leo played, letting it resonate with their souls. These listeners would often leave, deeply moved and with a clear perspective on the paths they needed to take in their lives.

The secret behind these revelations lied not within Leo's music, but within the listeners themselves. Leo's violin was simply a trigger for them to uncover their instinctive wisdom, liberating their minds, unveiling their true desires and untapped potentials.

So goes the story, reflecting upon the importance of opening oneself to unconventional, imperceptible sources of knowledge, and finding clarity within one's own soul.

The Silent Guide

Within a dense forest lived a tribe, so ancient and secluded that their dialect was like a cryptic code to outsiders. One day, a zealous explorer, set foot in the forest, determined to learn the tribe's secret language. He came across an old tribesman and sought to memorize the verbal exchange among the tribesfolk.

Months turned into years but the explorer could barely muster a comprehensible sentence. Frustrated and disheartened, he decided to depart from the mystic woods. As he packed his belongings, a half-blind, mute tribeswoman sensed his sadness, gestured him to follow her and led him to a secluded space in the forest.

She dug out a dusty, old scroll from beneath an ancient tree trunk, signifying that it was a map of the forest. Studying it, the explorer found strange, cryptic signs that seemingly held the key to the forest's long-lost secrets. Over time, he began to understand the tribe's language not through verbal exchange, but through symbols, signs and subtle gestures that were reflected in the map.

This parable teaches us that knowledge, even the most complex, is not always accessible through conventional means. Sometimes, the answers lie within us, waiting to be unleashed when we embrace silence, open our minds, and tune into the symphony of the soul.

The Inward Voyage

There was an experienced sailor who had conquered violent storms, battled fierce sea creatures, and navigated through treacherous waters. However, whispers remained of an elusive island in the center of the boundless sea. Driven by indomitable spirit, the sailor embarked on a quest to find it.

Through tumultuous storms and deceptive calm, the sailor searched in vain. One day, underneath the cerulean sky, he sat upon the calm water, frustrated. After a deep sigh, he closed his eyes, and suddenly he perceived the island, not on the exterior horizon, but within himself - a tranquil haven, a hidden treasure. Upon opening his eyes, the sailor realized what he had sought all along was an inward voyage; a journey into self-discovery.

The Silent Confidant

In a bustling city dwelled a quiet bookstore owner named Milton. He held within himself an uncanny wisdom, welcoming waves of customers into his humble store, not with words, but with his calming aura. Often, customers turned to him seeking advice, as though he was their silent confidant. Yet, Milton never instructed. Instead, he directed them towards certain books, seemingly tailored to their predicaments.

To a grieving widow, he offered a book on healing; to an uncertain student, he proffered philosophy; to an anxious parent, he suggested a tale of patience. Each found solace not in Milton's words, but in understanding the message behind the books he recommended. In truth, Milton shared deep wisdom without uttering a single word, guiding people not to answers but towards their own inner knowing.

A Guide in the Echoing Silence

A mountaineer set out on a great journey to conquer a colossal peak. The mountain whispered tales of danger, of courage, and of the many who failed. As he ascended, the mountaineer heard the echo of his own footsteps. This echoing silence served as his only guide in the deafening vastness.

When the path became treacherous, the quiet footsteps urged wisdom, when the icy cold bit, they kindled courage. It was if these echoes were discerning; mirroring his heart's desires, fears, and the mountain's challenges. By acknowledging his inner murmurs mirrored in the echoes, the mountaineer was able to conquer the peak. Triumphantly he realized, the greatest guide had been the dialogue within.

The Willful Current

A graceful river twisted and turned, coursing through forests, mountains, and valleys. It flowed with a willful current, rushing towards the mighty ocean. One day, the curious river asked the whispering wind, 'How does it feel to be free and unrestricted, going wherever you please?' The wind hummed, 'Every direction is my abode, but I am never home.'

The conversation turned the river quiet. It recognized its current's pull, not a constraint, but a guide, leading it home, to the ocean. The river realized freedom was not about aimlessly wandering, but about being guided by the inner pull, towards fundamental nature itself.

The Intuitive Key

Once upon a time in a small village lived a locksmith, known far and wide for his incredible ability to craft the finest keys and solve peculiar lock situations. His secret was the strange, ebony key he always carried with him. He proclaimed this was the 'Intuitive Key'. Unlike other keys, it seemed to have no set shape or form, instead, it appeared to adjust itself to fit any lock it came into contact with.

The townsfolk grew curious. They asked, 'Dear locksmith, tell us the secret of this intuitive key'. The locksmith answered, 'The key does not possess intelligence. Rather, it's receptive and adaptable. It understands and molds itself as per the need of the lock'.

The curious observer then concluded that the intuitive key indeed represents our inner voice, the voice that adjusts and tells the solutions once we allow it to be receptive to the problem at hand.

Uncanny Tale of the Silent Voice

In a forgotten corner of the world, there were people who lived in serene silence. These people were born mute but compensated for it with their heightened sense of understanding. There was one young chap, notoriously known for his ability to comprehend even the hidden messages in the silence. People named him the 'Silent Voice'.

Everyone wondered, 'How can a boy born without the gift of speech interpret messages with such precision?' The Silent Voice smiled and wordlessly pointed towards his heart. Baffled, people moved on.

It took them a while to realize that the 'Silent Voice' was his heart's voice which was quiet on the outside but spoke volumes within. And through understanding this voice, he began to perceive what otherwise was unseen.

Noiseless Navigational Voice

In a dense, foggy forest, a humble ant lived. The fog was so thick that the ant could not see where it was going. Other animals relied on their sight, and thus frequently ended up lost, or worse, trapped in spider webs or the claws of prowling predators.

To move around, the ant did not rely on sight, but instead, it was guided by an unseen but distinctly felt whisper of nature. It would feel tremors of the earth, perceive differences in humidity, and notice the subtle scents of trees and plants. These unspoken languages were the ant's map, even though they were silent to the rest of the world.

In our lives, we often find ourselves in situations resembling that foggy forest. Visibility is low, and the voices of the world are loud and distracting. Here, it is crucial to find that noiseless voice from within, allowing it to be our unseen navigational system to guide us through the fog.

Water's Invisible Messages

A sheppard in a drought-ridden land tended to his flock, always searching for a patch of green grass amidst the parched surroundings. Suddenly, he noticed a curious behaviour in a stray lamb that would aid the survival of his entire flock.

The lamb, despite his tender age, always lead the flock to patches of healthy grass. Observing the lamb, the sheppard noticed that it would bend its ear to the ground, and after sometime, lead the direction. The sheppard realised that the lamb was tuned into the faint whispers left by water that ran deep beneath the earth, a language unseen but perfectly understood by the lamb.

Similarly, we often overlook our own inner wisdom and innate ability to decipher the unseen messages of our life. Trust in these invisible signals is like finding water in a dry land, a guide through challenging times.

The Unheard Sound within the Shell

A seashore sculptor had the unique talent of carving extraordinary idols from seashells. Intricate, stunning work that seemed almost impossible to craft from such fragile material. When asked about his magical talent, he revealed his secret.

Before carving each shell, he would hold it close to his ears, listening for many silent moments. In the hush-hush whispers of the seashell, he understood its story, its strong parts, and its vulnerabilities. Thus, he was able to carve extraordinary forms without a single crack or chafe.

Similarly, when we tune into the silent voice within us, we gain insights into our strengths and weaknesses. This internal ear to hear the unheard guides us smoothly through the delicate art of living, enabling us to carve our own beautiful life journey without cracking under the world's pressures.

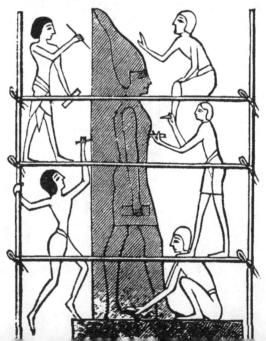

Eye of the Heart

There was once a young monk named Jin, who had been blind since he was a boy. Despite his visual impairment, he was renowned in his village for his uncanny ability to perceive things that others could not.

The villagers often marvelled at Jin's ability and asked him, 'Jin, how do you know so much without seeing?'. To which Jin would respond, 'By using the eyes of my heart.'

One day, a notable artiste from a neighbouring town heard of Jin and visited him. He brought a painting of a magnificent dawn, and asked Jin to describe it. Jin gently touched the canvas and after a moment of serenity, began to describe the scene with such vivacity that the artiste was astounded. He proclaimed, 'You've painted the painting into words with the brushes of your soul. Your heart's vision is truly divine.'

Hidden Voices of Insight

In a bustling city brimming with noise and chaos lived a violinist whose music resonated with unrivaled harmony. The violinist knew the secret of passing through the cacophony to extract melodies. Many visited this city, perplexed, asking the violinist, 'how do you discover these tunes amidst the clamor?'

The violinist answered with a smile, 'the melodies are always there, humming in the quiet depth, hidden beneath the distractions.' He would draw the bow across the violin strings, pulling forth notes that danced in perfect harmony, despite the commotion around them. People marveled at his ability, yet they failed to understand that the melodies the violinist played were the hidden voices of insight they too could hear if they allowed themselves to go past the surface uncertainties and look deeper.

Sacred Silent Cues

In a thriving forest, there thrived a mighty tree known among the forest-folk as 'Wise Oak.' The tree was ancient, its story interlaced within the threads of time. Every season, 'Wise Oak' demonstrated a peculiar behavior - it would shed a single leaf before the changing seasons, long before any other changes were evident. The forest dwellers who noticed this wondered why 'Wise Oak' seemingly knew ahead of time.

The truth lay not in what the tree did but in what it felt and perceived. The tree had mastered the art of sensing the smallest shifts in the wind's pattern and the subtle changes in temperature, far too slight for anything else to sense so early. The sacred silent cues from nature itself guided 'Wise Oak.' If observed, it would notice the tree's early signs of seasonal transition, appreciate its inherent wisdom and, perhaps, learn a thing or two about subtlety in the world's never-ending dialogue.

The Invisible Speaker's Tale

In the heart of a bustling market square stood a talking statue. Every day, at the strike of noon, it would regale the onlookers with captivating stories. But once a year, it would stay silent. Instead of a captivating story, the air would be filled with an invisible speech. The market would pause, curiosity pricking the air.

The wise among the crowd would close their eyes and let the unseen speaker weave a tale in their minds. An immersive saga of feelings, instincts, thoughts blossoming from silence. The invisible speaker told no story, yet its tale was more insightful than anything the statue narrated. The undistracted understood the language of the invisible speaker. They returned annually, not for the statue's stories, but for the silent tale that followed, knowing the greatest wisdom came from the depths of silence, apprehended only by the quiet listener.

Silent One's Revelation

Once, a young disciple trained under the watchful eye of an ancient sage. The sage was known for his wisdom but was even more renowned for his quiet demeanour. He spoke less, but whenever he did, his words were like precious jewels. The disciple, eager to imbibe the wisdom of his master, pressed him incessantly to share more.

One day, in response to the persistent requests, the sage pointed at a dormant volcano. He told the disciple that the mighty mountain was similar to his own wisdom. While it seemed inactive on the surface, a profound energy churned within its core.

The disciple, initially perplexed, started observing the volcano with a fervent curiosity. He realised that the volcano's tranquillity was not a symbol of stillness but a beacon of watchfulness, waiting for the perfect instance to unleash its tremendous energy. It was then he understood the sage's wisdom: external silence often cloaks a deep internal dialogue, echoing the voice of intuition.

Inner Light's Path

In the shimmering kingdom of the fireflies, there was a single lantern bearer. Tasked with lighting up the path for all the other fireflies, he used to burn himself brightly so others could traverse the forest with ease.

With passing time, the lantern bearer started to dim. Torn by his duty and the diminishing light, he began to question his purpose.

In his despair, he met a wise elder firefly who asked him to look within. Perplexed by the elder's advice, he decided to retreat to a secluded part of the forest.

In isolation, he discovered a spark, a faint glow deep within himself that had been invisible before because of his own bright light. This self-sourced illumination became a beacon, guiding him back to his purpose but with newfound wisdom: that the pathway to personal truth often lies in our own inner radiance, highlighted in solitude, mirroring the subtle pull of intuition.

The Silent Whisper

Once there lived a determined gold miner named Alf. He would toil day and night, searching for precious nuggets but often coming back empty-handed. One night, he dreamt of a soft whisper guiding him to the north side of the mountain, a path he had never taken before which seemed barren. He woke up and laughed at his silly dream. He was an experienced miner, and intuition had no role in this scientific pursuit.

Determined to prove the dream false, Alf ventured towards the north side despite his own reservations. To his shock, he discovered a generous vein of gold, much abundant than any he had found before. That day, Alf understood the power of the silent whisper, guiding him even in his sleep, and he began to give it more attention.

Henceforth, whenever he felt a tug, a whisper without sound, Alf would follow it. It wasn't always the easiest path, but it always bore gold, not always tangible, but of a kind that made him a richer man, in spirit and wisdom. His learned comrades chided his irrational ways until they saw the gleam in his eyes and the richness of his life. They realized that sometimes, the silent whisper could guide them to treasures beyond their wildest imagination.

Sage's Invisible Companion

In a secluded monastery in the Himalayas, lived a wise old sage, known for his unparalleled wisdom. However, one peculiarity intrigued everyone - the sage, during his daily routines, would pause at random moments, close his eyes, and appear to be listening to something utterly invisible. Confounded, they sought answers.

The sage explained, 'I have an invisible companion. Whenever I am on the brink of a decision, big or small, I pause and listen to this companion.' The students were intrigued, 'How do we find our invisible companions?' 'A silent mind and an open heart,' replied the sage.

From then on, the students practiced silence and openness. As they honed this, they began to perceive their own invisible companions. It wasn't in the form of a tangible presence but a distinct echo, an inner voice. Making decisions became easier for them, ultimately transforming the monastery into a place brimming with wisdom and contentment.

The Elixir of Intuition

Far in the great mountains, there lived a monk known for his wisdom and his brew, the 'Elixir of Intuition', believed to awaken one's senses to new panoramas of understanding. Many travel afar to experience this magical elixir.

A scholar, desiring to experience this magical potion, made the difficult journey to the monk's hermitage. Upon arrival, the monk served him a brew, nothing more than a concoction of ordinary herbs and honey.

The scholar exclaimed, 'This isn't magical at all!' The monk gently smiled, 'The brew is not magical. It merely prompts you to still your mind. In the state of calmness, what blossoms within you is your intuition, and that's the only magic you need'.

Voice of the Heart

A famed Samurai, known for his bravery, always won his battles. However, an obscure battle found him bested, not by a stronger adversary but a frail old woman. The warrior, humiliated yet desperate to learn, asked how she, with such less power, could win.

'It is the voice of the heart,' she said, 'It whispered to me when to duck, when to strike, and when to hold back.' Intrigued, he asked her to elaborate. 'It takes a lifetime to master but can be started in a moment,' the woman explained. 'You have to learn to listen, truly listen to the throbbing heart within you. When you can hear its voice distinctly, your body shall follow its guidance without hesitation.'

The Samurai, after that day chose to meditate rather than practice brute force. As the days passed, he grew quieter but stronger, as he trained himself to listen to the subtle guidance of his heart. In his future battles, he not just conquered his enemies but also the storm brewing within him.

Embedded Insight: Unveiling the Hidden

A sharp-eyed falcon soared high in the azure expanse, searching below for its sustenance. This majestic bird, known through the kingdom for its keen sight, struggled to find a morsel in the vast landscape stretched beneath.

In its flight, the falcon noticed a small oakling, meek and humble. Unlike the proud trees towering around, this tiny oakling seemed inconsequential. However, the falcon, desperate and weary, decided to descend anyway.

As it landed next to the unassuming sapling, it noticed subtle oscillations beneath the earth. Opening its beak, it unearthed a nest of grubs hidden deep within the ground; a feast it would never have discovered from its high vantage point.

The little falcon, in spite of its might and vision, had unsheathed wisdom from a source meek in appearance; teaching us that our deepest understanding often springs from places unseen, whispering to us in a language as quiet as intuition.

Echoes of the Unseen

In a town nestled by a river, a curious musician named Elias lived. He was drawn to the unseen, the echoes that wafted in the stillness between the moment and its next. One day, he saw a rare instrument, Aeolia, a wind harp that played melody without human touch. Elias eagerly purchased Aeolia, setting it up in his home by the river.

Months passed, and Elias failed to hear Aeolia's song, for the town was perpetually bustling. Dismayed, he turned towards other pursuits, yet he never put Aeolia away. One silent night, while immersed in his thoughts, Elias heard a subtle tune. Aeolia was playing, its sounds shaped by the nightly breeze. After that, Elias found his heartbeat synced to Aeolia's rhythm, the song would play in the quietest hours, urging him to follow its song to compose beautiful music.

The echoes of the unseen, thus, were not apparent amongst the jumbling clamour but in the silence. Elias found the essence of Aeolia's creation was not force, but the indirect inspiration it cast in the silent moments. Unseen it remained, but his life felt its influence.

The Gentle Nudge

In vast prairies, there lived a wise honeybee, popularly known for her ability to detect the sweetest nectar amidst a sea of blossoms. The secret to her flair was a gentle nudge she felt in her wings whenever she hovered close to the right flower.

As the prairie bloomed each spring, various flowers filled the air with enticing fragrances. But amid all that blooming confusion, the wise honeybee relied on that gentle nudge. Each direction she considered, she would pause, waiting for that feeling, and when it came, she would take flight assured. It never led her astray.

The gentle nudge, henceforth, was her compass in the riot of spring, the refined awareness that guided her to the sweetest nectar. Amid many possibilities, she found the best choice by paying attention to that delicate shift in her wings.

Secrets of the Silent Guide

In an ancient kingdom, there was a noble knight called Theodore. His acclaimed prowess wasn't solely from his physical strength but also from his silent guide. A guide unknown to everyone, but Theodore himself. It was an inner assist that glowed brighter when he was on the right course.

He recalled its first appearance as a child while choosing between toy soldiers. A peculiar glow led him to the finest one. Theodore followed his silent guide in knightly duels, complex negotiations, and daunting quests. Through practice, he learned to lay still, letting his mind calm to perceive his silent guide's glow, revealing the path he needed.

Theodore's silent guide led him to remarkable triumphs, and he treasured this silent companion. It was a beacon only he could perceive, it was not loud or forceful. Yet, its directions yielded harmony beyond what was externally obvious.

Quiet Impulse: A Tale of Direction

Along the shoreline lived a skilled sailor, Marigold. She had an uncanny knack for predicting the next day's weather. Not from traditional methods but an instinct, a quiet impulse inside her that hinted at the morrow's waves.

She would watch the setting sun, feel the breeze and the silence beneath, and there it was, that quiet impulse. It pulled her understanding towards the most likely prediction for next day's weather. Her forecasts were near flawless, earning her merchant ships' trust, who relied on her word to schedule their ventures.

Over time, Marigold understood that her quiet impulse wasn't conjured up by forceful thinking but appeared in moments of deep tranquility. In the hush of her heart, she found a guidance that spoke volumes, confirmed in the winds and waves of each day's dawn.

The Silent Drumbeat

Once, in a village compact with musicians, lived a wise drummer named Mafu. His drum was considered magical, for each beat displayed an array of emotions, capable of making anyone dance or weep. However, his drumbeat stopped abruptly one day. Stress clouded the village as the constant rhythm that paced their life halted. Everyone tried beating the drum, but it remained silent.

One day, a young lad named Thabo ignored everyone's ridicule to give the drum a try. Thabo was deaf and couldn't hear the drumbeat even when it was at its prime. Thabo gently placed the drum in his lap and closed his eyes. Feeling the drum with his palms, he perceived the tiniest of vibrations. He rhythmically moved his fingers on the drum, aligned with these vibrations. To the village's astonishment, the drum started beating again, not loud, but subtly, resonating with an unparalleled beauty.

Thabo taught the villagers a profound lesson that day. True music isn't just about hearing the loud beats but about acknowledging the silent rhythm that has always been there, the small voice that shakes us from our core.

Inaudible Signals

In the heart of a dense forest lived a tribe that had never been touched by modern technology. No radios, no televisions, just the harmonious stream of nature's sound. Each tribe member had an unusual bond with a bird that sent them signals about upcoming weather, imminent danger, or food availabilities.

One young man, Sefa, struggled as his bird was speechless. Frustrated, he complained to the elder. The elder smiled and advised Sefa to spend more time with his bird. Even without understanding, Sefa paid heed and started observing his bird. Days turned into weeks, and he noticed the bird would flap its wings in a certain pattern, slightly twitch his head, or sway in a peculiar way, each meaning different things.

Eventually, Sefa became the most adept in the tribe at reading signals, not from the bird's sound, but from its subtle movements. He demonstrated that sometimes the valuable cues in life are not always auditory but can be present in understated, silent gestures.

Moon's Secret Teachings

In a kingdom under the silver glow of the moon, a curious boy named Eze lived. He constantly wondered about the moon's phases. How did the moon know when to grow full and when to vanish into the skies? His curiosity led him to spend countless nights observing the lunar dance under the sky's vast canvas.

Eze realized the moon, even in its smallest crescent or its imperceptible presence, was actually whole. The shadow merely hid the truth which, given patience and time, bared itself completely. Inspired by the moon, Eze decided to let this phenomenon guide his life. Whenever faced with a difficult decision, he would take a step back, observe, patient like the moon, until the right path revealed itself.

He realized that just like the ever-whole moon, the answer is always within us. We merely need patience and trust in our internal guiding light for the answer to manifest. The moon, with its shifting silhouettes, taught Eze to believe in his inherent wholeness and inner wisdom.

Resounding Silence

Many years ago, in a remote town, lived an old and wise cello player, acclaimed for his enthralling melodies. However, one day he announced his retirement due to his deteriorating hearing ability. The townsfolk were deeply disheartened, they decided to present him a golden tuning fork for his years of contribution.

The gift was to honor his past accomplishments, but the old man saw potential in it. He began placing the tuning fork on the cello to feel the vibrations of the music he could no longer hear. He found that the more still his own heart and mind were, the more nuanced the cello's vibrations he could feel. Surprisingly, he started playing again, entrancing the audience with his stunning music, heard and unheard—bringing joy to their hearts.

Through his golden tuning fork, he learned and demonstrated that even when one's traditional means of understanding might fade, there is always another path available, sometimes even richer in its guidance. In silence, he amplified the power of the unobserved, the intangible vibrations of wisdom, and the music of the heart.

Knowing the Unseen

In a remote kingdom known for its breathtaking landscapes, there lived a renowned sculptor named Elion. One day, he was commissioned by the king to sculpt a magnificent statue from a raw slab of marble. The king, intrinsically impatient, wanted the statue to be ready in an impossible time frame. However, Elion didn't verbalize his resistance but merely nodded.

Nobody understood how Elion could take on such an impossible task. But Elion had a unique gift. It wasn't that he could sculpt quickly or efficiently, though his hands were skillful indeed. His gift was the ability to 'see' what others couldn't. When looking at a slab of marble, he could see the statue it could become.

Days turned into weeks. Weeks stretched into months. The king, growing impatient, shouted at Elion, 'How much longer will it take?' Elion, in steady demeanor, replied, 'The statue is already there within the marble, sire. We must simply reveal it.' Elion carried on his work, trusting the image reflected in his inner vision. The completed statue was unveiled just in time and was of such astonishing beauty that it left the kingdom speechless. Elion listened inwardly and understood things others couldn't even see.

Silent Raindrop's Course

In the vast canvas of the azure sky, a single raindrop embarked upon a journey towards the ground. Countless gusts of winds blew, each trying to redirect the raindrop in various directions. But the raindrop held its course. It didn't fight against the raging tempests, nor did it change its path based on the flighty winds' persuasions.

Observing this spectacle from his home was a hermit who lived in seclusion. Intrigued by the raindrop's course, he said to himself, 'It knows not words of warning nor promises of encouragement, yet it travels the right path.' The hermit realized that like the raindrop, he too had a course charted out in his heart. There were plenty who tried to redirect him, but his inner 'calling,' silent like a raindrop's course, guided him better.

The Inaudible Roar

Deep in the jungle lived a lion, feared and respected by all creatures for his might. Unexpectedly, a severe illness took the lion's roar away, leaving him in utter silence. The animal kingdom saw an opportunity in the lion's weakness and started challenging his reign. Desperate, the lion retreated to his den, hoping for recovery but feeling defeated.

One day, as he lay in silence, he felt a different kind of roar within him. Though it made no sound, it stirred emotions, summoned willpower, and ignited a flame of determination. The lion started venturing out, facing his challengers without a roar, defeating them with sheer power, courage and quiet confidence.

Soon, the entire jungle took notice of the silent yet intimidating presence of the lion. They realized that the lion's true roar wasn't a sound, but the indomitable strength and courage emanating from within. The lion's 'inaudible roar,' a guiding force from deep within, made him stronger than ever.

Quill's Silent Inscriptions

A story-teller was known throughout the city for recounting tales through beautiful vast canvases. His works were breathtaking, brimming with vibrant colors and countless inscriptions within the strokes. However, the quill with which he created these masterpieces never made a sound.

One day, a curious onlooker said, 'Why does your quill write in silence? Wouldn't the beauty of music or pleasant words enhance your art?' The artist replied, 'My quill inscribes the voices whispered into my empathy, the visions felt in my spirit, and the emotions that roar in quietude within my heart. Although it doesn't make a sound, without it, my stories would never reach the canvas.'

The silent inscriptions made by the artist's quill served as a reminder. The true beauty of expression often lies in the quietest corners of our souls, where intuition whispers its soft guidance.

The Solitary Conductor

In the quiet town of Maestoso, everyone knew of the solitary conductor. A man who, despite his loneliness, created the sweetest symphony one could ever hear. They said he had an unusual skill; he didn't need an orchestra. Every instrument under his baton was the rustling leaves, the whispering wind, the trickling brook, the chirping birds.

The townsfolk wondered, 'How does he do it? How does he compose such celestial melodies with no musicians?' For they saw him only waving his baton, the enchanting musical notes enveloping them mysteriously. Finally, one day, a curious boy from the town gathered enough courage to ask the conductor.

'How do you command things that can't speak, to produce such beautiful music?' The conductor looked at him then glanced towards the sky, listening intently. He then turned back and said, 'Every rustle, every ripple, every tweet is a note, my young friend. The instruments are all around us. To create a symphony one doesn't need more musicians but more attention. Open your senses, not your assumptions, and you'll hear the music I hear.'

The Undertone of Certainty

A scholar from the kingdom of Prospera was well known for his wisdom. Despite his vast knowledge, he would often fall short in his predictions about the future of the kingdom. Each time his predictions failed, the King would say, 'Listen harder.'

One day, the scholar, confused and upset, asked the king, 'My lord, you always say 'Listen harder', but I've consumed all the books of knowledge in your kingdom. What more should I be listening to?'

The king smiled, walked up to the scholar and pointed towards the bustling market. 'Look towards the market, tell me what you hear?' said the king. The scholar replied, 'I hear haggling noises, laughter, the ringing of coins.'

The King quietly responded, 'And I hear plans, deals, aspirations and fears.' He turned to the scholar, 'It is not about more knowledge but understanding the undertone of certainty within the rhythm of life. That is where the truth lies.'

Wood's Whispered Secrets

Deep in the Emerald woods lived an old carpenter named Alden. Many came to him for his famous chairs; each one a masterpiece, mysteriously resonating comfort and ease that no other chair could produce. Anyone who sat in them could feel the stress melt away.

A young apprentice, fascinated by Alden's skills, asked, 'Master, how can you create such magic with mere wood and tools?'

Alden turned to his apprentice, smiling gently, 'Oh, it's not just wood and tools, lad. It's the whispers.' He tapped the wood fondly and continued, 'Each tree has a story. Can you hear it?'

The curious apprentice, listening closely, could only hear the sounds of the forest. Years later, the apprentice understood what Alden meant. Every creation speaks of its purpose. In the case of the chairs, it was to provide comfort. The ability to listen to that purpose, that whisper, was the secret to creating great things.

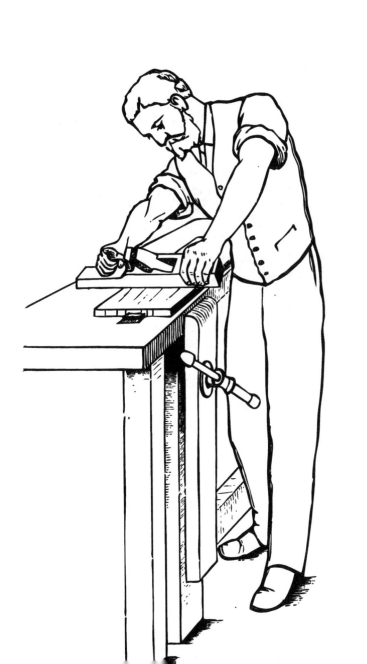

Unspoken Assurances

In Veritas, a town famous for its glassworks, lived a glassblower, famed for creating glassware so perfect, it seemed infused with divine magic. Among his creations were incredibly intricate glasses that, when filled with wine, were said to reveal the drinker's truthful soul.

When his apprentice asked how this was possible, the glassblower said, 'The glass speaks to me. Through its heat and the cold, its shape and its formlessness. It tells me how far it can bend, how much it can take, exactly where to touch so as not to break it.'

The apprentice, eager to learn, tried many times but always ended up with broken shards. One day, as he watched his master work, he noticed a certain stillness, a serene calm, a silence that belied intense focus and sensitivity. The glassblower was connecting with the glass, in an exquisite dance of creation and surrender.

In that moment, the apprentice understood. The master was not just blowing glass. He was extending unspoken assurances to the material, acknowledging its strength and understanding its fragility, thus creating magnificent masterpieces. The magic was in the silent empathetic connection.

The Wise Silence

Once upon a time, in a town bustling with noise, dwelt a renowned sage. Many came from far across the land, drawn by his wisdom, seeking his counsel. Yet, the sage never spoke. He nodded, he smiled, yet words from him were scarce. His followers were puzzled, did wisdom not espouse speaking? The wise ones, however, noticed that whenever the sage's silence enveloped them, they found the answer to their dilemmas.

They discovered that their chatter, their incessant questions, drowned their understanding. In the sage's silence, they learnt to quiet their minds, to become still. And in that stillness, they found a voice familiar yet unheard, hidden under the jangle of their thoughts, the voice of their heart whispering the truth.

Calm Depth of Revelation

Across the shimmering silver sea dwelt an elder shark. Despite his enormous size and power, he was known amongst the sea creatures as the contemplative one. Varieties of sea creatures would race, compete, arguing over tiny matters and generally creating a ruckus in the shallow waters. The other sea dwellers often wondered why this mighty shark preferred the silent and deep abyss.

One day, a curious young squid swam up to the elder shark. He questioned him on why he dwelt in the darkest depth while he could indulge in the merriment of the shallow waters. The elder shark, with a compassionate smile enveloping his face, calmly responded, 'When the tempests hit, the surface waters get turbulent, and its inhabitants scatter in fear and confusion. But here in the depth, all is calm, unchanging. Here, every heartbeat resonates clearly, enhancing my understanding about the very essence of life.'

The little squid, baffled at first, decided to join the shark. In the quiet, he found clarity striking like a lightning, allowing him to comprehend what the elderly shark meant - In the calm depth, lies the truth.

Whispering Impressions

Within a thick thriving forest, stood a colossal tree. It had sheltered generations of tiny forest beings, and constantly whispered to the wind. Hikers often noticed that surrounding this old being, the forest catered a peculiar silence, a quiet that commanded respect.

Once, an old traveler distressed by life's contradictions approached this tree seeking enlightenment. He sat under its shade and endlessly poured out his confusion in words. After a while, when he finally exhausted himself of words, he decided to rest. As he laid down, he noticed something unique, the wind passing through the tree's leaves whispered back to him.

The whispers, like delicate threads, entwined into the traveler's soul. In his quiet surrender, the whispering leaves brought forth answers to his questions. It was then he realized, it was not the wind whispering, but his soul echoing back at him. The answers, all this while, were hidden within him waiting to be unveiled.

Silent Heartstrings

In the world of melodies, dwelt a violin, exquisitely crafted, known for its melodious charm. It had always amazed orchestras with its harmonious tunes, yet it sometimes uttered a distinctive soft note, unheard by the busy orchestra or the pleased audience.

The soft note would only appear when the violin was alone in silence, with the echo of the past melody still lingering in the air.

Once, a young luthier happened upon this note. He was struck by its magic and decided to recreate the note, but all his attempts were futile. He tinkered with strings, the bow, but the magic remained unrecreated. Frustrated, he surrendered, laying the violin in silence.

In the calm moment of surrender, he heard an echo of the note, the innocent tune danced around him, whispering words of wisdom that the magic is not in the change of physical elements but in the silence and calmness of the heart. This mystical note arose from the violin's connection with its deeper self, its intuition emanating as a melody.

Between the Lines of Reality

In a quaint village resided a famed artist, celebrated for her masterpieces that spoke beyond colors and figures. Her studio was filled with a vast range of colors, but the black and white paints were the most used. Individuals from far and wide marveled at the subtle influences behind her art.

One curious admirer inquired, 'Why do you paint largely in black and white, given the range of colors you possess?' The artist responded with a loving smile, 'Colors indeed are beautiful but the true essence of life lies in the contrast of black and white.'

'Black represents life's hardships; white signifies the triumphs. Look deeper into my paintings; they express the untold, capturing the essence you feel but seldom understand. That stirring is your inner voice guiding you, much like the black-white balance guides my art.'

In the artist's explanation, her admirer found a profound comprehension of their innate guide, gently navigating them through life's shades of complexities.

The Inner Eye Opens

In a small town, there lived a skillful sculptor, known for his impeccable statues. Each sculpture held a life of its own, reflecting the sculptor's intuitive connection with his creations. However, he was oblivious to his sense of inherent wisdom and attributed his talent entirely to his practiced craft.

However, an incident occurred that made him question his rational deductions. A noble commissioned him to sculpt a life-sized statue of his daughter. While the reference painting displayed a smiling, vibrant lady, the sculptor's inner vision saw sadness and longing in her eyes. He was torn between the expectation and his gut feeling.

Finally, he trusted his inner eye and highlighed the unexpressed melancholy through his creation. When he unveiled the sculpture, the silence in the room dropped heavy as a stone. The noble stepped forward, tears welling up in his eyes. 'Never has anyone captured my daughter's spirit so well, her hidden sorrow so perfectly.', he whispered.

The incident opened the sculptor's inner eye, enabling him to perceive the unspoken, to understand the untold, and to craft immortal masterpieces. From that day forth, he learned to confide in his instincts, letting them guide his creations.

Whispers in the Wind

In a distant kingdom, a young alchemist, Meiran, was tasked with a critical mission- to find the secret ingredient for the elixir of wisdom. The elders told him that the answer lies within the wind, 'listen to its whispers and let it guide you,' they said.

For months, Meiran would station himself high on the hills attempting to comprehend the language of the wind. He was expecting to hear clear instructions or a precise answer, but all he heard were incomprehensible whispers and rustling leaves. Despaired and perplexed, Meiran decided to return to the kingdom empty-handed.

But as he descended the hill, a gush of wind whistled past his ears, and for the first time, the wind's hum didn't seem as foreign. He had no verbal explanation, but something within relished on the gusty melody, a feeling of certainty arose within, making him follow a path seldom taken.

The path led him to a valley abundant with plants he had never seen. Amongst them, a luminescent herb drew his attention. He took it back to the kingdom. After understanding its properties, he found the missing ingredient.

The wind had whispered no words, yet it guided Meiran, answering his quest. The whispers in the wind were nothing but the silent language of his intuition, guiding him upon the path less traveled.

The Silent Guide Within

A sculptor named Artimelios lived in the heart of the city. He was renowned for his exquisite sculptures, incomparable to any other in his town. People often asked him about his secret.

One day, a pupil decided to stay after class, eager to learn. 'Master, tell me, how do you breathe life into lifeless stone?' Artimelios looked at the young boy and smiled. 'There's a silent guide within me,' he replied, 'it leads my hands.'

The pupil, mystified, thought Artimelios was hiding his secret. He searched for books that would explain this 'silent guide' but found nothing. After going through countless scrolls and scriptures, he decided to confront Artimelios.

Seeing the exhausted boy, Artimelios led him to a block of stone. 'Pick up chisel and hammer, give this stone a form,' he said. The boy tried but ended up creating a misshapen figure. Frustrated, he threw down the tools, 'I can't do it!'

'Close your eyes, silence your mind. Let the stone tell you what it wants to be. Don't guide the chisel; let the chisel be guided. Trust the unspoken direction.' The boy did as he was told. Hours later, he brought forth a beautiful sculptured bird from the stone.

'This is the silent guide within,' smiled Artimelios. This encounter taught the pupil that his silent guide was his intuition, giving his hand the wisdom to shape his masterpiece from the stone.

Invisible Murmurs

There was a master carpenter who was known for creating magnificent masterpieces. His work wasn't dictated by external blueprints but a unique inner compass seemed to guide his hands. He once told his apprentices, 'You must listen to the wood, it will reveal what it wishes to become.'

The apprentices were bewildered by the master's words. Nevertheless, one of them decided to apply such peculiar advice. He held a piece of wood, closed eyes and listened. Days turned into weeks. The apprentice heard nothing, and frustration crept in.

On the brink of giving up, the apprentice murmured, 'Speak to me.' The response did not come from the wood, but from within himself, an idea so brilliant that he was taken aback. Through his inner voice, he crafted an exquisite piece that became legendary. He realized the wisdom in the carpenter's words; the murmurs were not from the wood, but an echo of his intuitive voice that guided his masterpiece.

Songs from the Inner Depths

Long ago, in a town known for its music, lived an odd musician. While others played popular tunes, his music was different, as it came from a place deep within him. His music wasn't loud or cheerful, yet it had a strong resonance that touched people's hearts.

In a grand concert, the musician showcased his exceptional skills. His strange, silent start had the audience in an expectant hush. The crowd was perplexed as he closed his eyes, seemingly lost in thought. When a beautiful melody started, the audience felt each note vibrating with an intense profundity.

When asked by an enchanted audience member about his inspiration, the musician answered, 'I create symphonies from the silent tunes humming within my soul. It is an internal conversation, a song, my unconscious mind sings to me. I simply translate it into music.' Through his songs, the musician taught many that the most beautiful orchestrations come from the depths of our consciousness, our intuitive song that awaits its tune.

Footsteps in the Dark

Once upon a timeless night, a blindfolded man was guided to traverse a thick forest. No retainer of sight, no baton, only faith in his senses and the mysterious whispers of the trees.

One evening, he had forgotten his standard path. He paused, consciousness echoing in the unknown like bare feet in quiet seclusion. While others might have lost hope, he drummed faith in his heartbeats and proceeded further, groping his way through the whispering darkness.

Slowly over time, his senses became familiar with the rhythm of the unseen landscape. The crunching leaves underfoot were his script, the wind brushing against the trees – his canvas, the scent of blooming flowers his guidance. He became a composer in an orchestra of unspoken cacophonies, his silent footsteps shaping symphonies in the dim void.

In his persistent journey, he had discovered uncharted routes, feeling his way amidst the darkness, scripting a path of his own. Thus, the blindfolded man, enveloped in darkness, discovered the potency of his senses, understanding that silence sometimes resonates louder than clamours, unveiling rhythms unheard to an undistracted ear.

Chorus of the Unheard

In a harmonious woodland, each creature lent its voice to the daily orchestration of life. But there was an outcast amongst them, a mute swan whose silence echoed louder than any songbird.

While the mirthful consortium painted sonnets in the azure, she lingered in reflective solitude, bearing a melancholy silence. But within this silence resonated an uncanny wisdom, a chorus of the unheard, whispering subtle truths.

She navigated through the woodland, understanding every rustle of leaves, every secret sigh of the wind, every rush of the stream. Her harmony lay not in her voice but in the wisdom she imbibed from her surrounding symphony.

The mute swan taught the woodland rhythms their true essence, for she proved that the choir of life wasn't just about lending your voice to the ensemble but about understanding and participating in the music, even in silence. Consequently, in the woodland's chorus of life, her silent wisdom echoed the loudest.

Hidden Scrolls of Insight

In the city of ancient Alexandria, lay hidden the greatest library of the time. The library had an exceptional set of scrolls, called the 'Scrolls of Insight'. Tales spoke of their ability to provide the reader the knowledge they sought the most. Those who read it found their destinies shaping as per their deepest inquiries.

An outsider, after hearing this tale, felt drawn towards it. With the librarian's permission, he was allowed to read these scrolls but warned not to
misjudge them as ordinary parchments.

As he began reading, he saw just abstract symbols and shapes bearing no meaning. Over time, he realized that these scrolls were reflecting his own subconscious fears and desires; and as he learned to understand these reflections, his path became more and more evident. The scrolls, indeed, were no magical entity, but the mirror to one's own intuition.

The Elusive Current

In the seclusion of a closed room, a camphor flame flickered. The flame, neither fidgeting nor dimming, burned with the grace of a lotus in bloom – unmoved by the turbulent breeze outside.

When a gust of wind seeped into the room through a half-open window, the other elements danced and shivered. The parchments rustled, the curtains waved, and the dust spiraled. But the flame stood still, flickering quietly as it mirrored the tranquil stream flowing in the cavern of its heart.

Despite the turmoil outside, the flame embodied poise, creating an aura where silence and wisdom danced together. This wisdom wasn't a whispered secret or a cryptic puzzle but an elusive current flowing through the everyday clamors – waiting to be perceived by an open heart, serene enough to listen.

Thus, the flame taught the lesson of silent wisdom, echoing the value of calm introspection in the face of turbulence. For intuitive guidance, one doesn't need to seek answers in the noise. Instead, in the silence lies the elusive current of truth, if only one stills his wind-tossed mind to perceive it.

Intrinsic Rhythms of Wisdom

In the heart of a temporal realm existed a timeless entity – a mystical drum. This Drum of Eternity performed, dictated not by any musician but by the Divine itself.

Each beat echoed an eternal truth in a language beyond human tongues, resonating serenely in the cosmic space. Though its rhythms were visible to all, only those who still their mind and feel its echo truly understood the language of its drumbeats.

A cacophony reigned in the realm, where inhabitants sought wisdom. They failed to understand that the orchestra of life wasn't about creating tumultuous notes but about listening - to perceive the silent rhythms beating under the bustling surface.

The Drum of Eternity taught the inhabitants a significant truth: wisdom isn't about seeking noise to drown other sounds. Instead, aligning yourself harmoniously with the intrinsic rhythms of the universe lets you decipher the deepest truths, resonating louder than any worldly clamor.

The Secret Pulse of Intuition

In an ancient city lived a skillful bell maker. His bells were treasured far and wide for their flawless tones. Yet, the bell maker was blind. Sightless, he relied on his intuition to decide when the molten metal was ready to be shaped.

Once poured, the bell would cool and his apprentices would examine it, finding no fault in form or sound. People wondered how he produced flawless bells without sight. When asked, he said he felt a pulse, an unspoken nudge, right before the molten metal reached its ideal state.

We all possess a deep-down pulse within us, a swaying of our heart against the normal rhythm when the time is right, or the decision perfect. This internal harmony, by nature's code of secrecy, is our intuition's pulse. Heeding this allows us to craft our own perfect bells in the foundries of life.

Unexplicit Tale of the Invisible Messenger

Once upon a time in a kingdom far, far away, there was a wise king who had an uncanny ability to predict events, seemingly out of the blue. His kingdom thrived under his care, advancing in all aspects, and sometimes it looked as though the king was receiving advice from an unseen entity.

Unbeknownst to his subjects, the king had mastered the art of receiving messages from the 'Invisible Messenger'. This Messenger was not an otherworldly spirit or an angel, but the king's inner voice. Whenever the king was in a tough spot, he would retreat to his chambers, away from the bustle of the court and the noise of his advisors. There, in silence, he would listen to that faint whisper in his mind, his Invisible Messenger guiding him towards the right decision.

At first, these messages were quiet whispers, barely audible amidst the noise of his thoughts. But the more the king listened, the clearer the voice became. Finally, the day came when the voice was as clear as any actual conversation. And with that, the king led his kingdom into a golden era of peace and prosperity.

Earth's Hidden Tunes

In a small village nestled between towering mountains and a glistening lake, lived an old man known for his dance. He had an uncanny knack for predicting the movements of nature. He would dance when there were no evident signs of an approaching storm, only for the heavens to break out into a wild downpour immediately. Sometimes, he'd stop suddenly in the middle of his chores and start a gentle sway, signifying the glory of the unseen sun behind thick clouds.

Secretly, the villagers often wondered how he could track the rhythm of Earth, unseen to their eyes and unheard by their ears. Little did they know, it was not because of extraordinary hearing ability, but through patience and deep internal listening that he found the 'hidden tunes' of the Earth.

As he listened to the wind, sensed changes in temperature, or felt vibrations in the Earth, he could hear an underlying rhythm that no one else could pick up. This was not an easier feat, but a gift nurtured over years of silent watchfulness, a reward for years of listening to the intuitive wisdom within.

The Untold Messages from Within

In the bustling city of Granderton, there lived a fearless detective, renowned for his uncanny knack of solving the most baffling mysteries. His secret weapon wasn't some ultra-modern gadgetry or cutting-edge technology. It was something everyone has, but seldom checks - an encrypted channel of untold messages from within.

Whenever he was presented with a case, he would retreat to his quiet study. In calming silence, he engaged his inner intuitive mind, seeking insights from within. With closed eyes, a relaxed mind, and receptive spirit, he would listen to that often unheard voice inside him.

An insightful whisper here, a hunch there, his intuition would weave together the most correlated reasons and twist them into a whole - unveiling truths that logical analysis alone would miss. His reliance on his intuitive guidance made him not just an extraordinary detective, but a beacon of wisdom in the city of Granderton.

Spirit's Silent Song

Suspended in the cosmos, was a desolate planet known as Valeska, home to a bare population of celestial beings who had a unique talent. Unlike humans, they didn't communicate through words, they 'listened' through subtle frequencies of their ethereal bodies. Their communication tool, their language, was their 'Spirit's Silent Song'.

This silent song spoke words that no language has the capacity to express. It was an echo of their inner narrative, a mirror of their deepest sentiments, desires, and wisdom. But to hear its melodious notes they would immerse themselves in peace and silence, to hush the chaos of their mental cosmos.

To these beings, their Silent Song held utmost clarity about their path, decisions, and actions. By yielding to this internal guide and tuning in to its frequency, they navigated their existence, evolved and encouraged others to listen to their own Spirit's Silent Song.

The Stone's Untold Story

There once was a sculptor known throughout the land for his grand pieces of art. However, he held a curious belief. He claimed that he was not the creator of his sculptures; rather the stone whispered its form to him. The village thought his idea strange, yet his magnificent sculptures were proof of his unusual talent.

Each time he was presented with a new block of marble, he would sit before it in silence. He would close his eyes, lay his hands upon the stone, and listen until the song of unseen art rang clear. Following the internal melody, he would carve and polish the marble until the creature hidden within was revealed.

His precision wasn't born from mere mastery over his craft, but from his genuine ability to listen. He did not force upon the stone a form of his choosing; he listened and allowed the stone's inner beauty to surface.

Moral of the Parable: Only when we silence our minds, letting go of preconceived notions and judgments, can we reveal the true form of our inner wisdom.

Unsaid Secrets Unveiled

A sage was known far and wide for his ability to predict the future. Kings, noblemen, and peasants alike would come to consult him, hoping to glimpse their destinies. They marveled at how he could derive accurate predictions from the most ordinary objects.

A curious scholar asked the sage one day, 'How, O wise one, are you able to read the future from something as mundane as a piece of cloth or a lump of soil?' The sage laughed and replied, 'The future is not written on these items. Rather, they communicate a language beyond words. It whispers, and I merely allow myself to understand.'

The scholar couldn't comprehend. The sage gestured towards a pot of blooming flowers and whispered, 'The flowers don't speak, yet they communicate the arrival of spring. Similarly, our hearts whisper secrets that our minds often ignore, drown in noise or confuse.'

Moral of the Parable: When we quieten our minds and open our hearts, the unsaid secrets of our intuition will make themselves known.

Wise Hum of the Depths

In a bustling harbor town lived an old fisherman. His catches were always plentiful, regardless of the unpredictable sea and the inexperienced younger fishermen often asked for his secret. The old fisherman would always reply with a twinkle in his eye, 'I listen to the sea.'

The younger fishermen did not understand; they too heard the sea, its waves and storms. Yet their nets often came back empty. The old fisherman laughed seeing their confused faces. He explained, 'You hear the sea, but you don't listen. The sea hums a tale each day; sometimes it tells of bounty, sometimes scarcity. I listen to her hum with an open heart and she guides me to her gifts.'

The young fishermen learned to quiet their minds and listen with clear hearts to the sea's whispers, and they too started reaping bountiful catches.

Moral of the Parable: When one learns to listen, the depth of wisdom can guide you to unexpected rewards.

Feather's Silent Flight

Within the heart of the rainforest, a brilliant parrot known for its vibrant plumage and robust calls lived on the highest tree. The parrot's sister, on the flip side, was simpler - carrying muted tones, and she barely made a sound. Her flight was as silent as the moon's dance across the night sky.

One day, an unexpected storm brewed. Tormented by the chaotic winds, the brilliant parrot couldn't keep his flight stable despite all his strength and vibrant colours. Meanwhile, his sister manoeuvred effortlessly, her delicate wings catching the wind currents, her silent flight an embodiment of seamless grace.

The turmoil revealed a truth: grace isn't always loud, nor strength always visible. True navigation through life's storms often requires a silent dance with the wind, honouring the soft guidance of intuition.

The Clandestine Guidebook

Within the royal library, there was rumored to be a powerful tome - The Clandestine Guidebook. This guidebook was said to hold the knowledge and answers to each person's unique life path. However, despite the extensive search by scholars and seekers, this book could never be found.

One day, an old librarian who had served the library for years overheard another failed expedition's complaints. The old librarian smiled and whispered, 'The Clandestine Guidebook cannot be found in the material world. It exists within us. It opens not with keys but with tranquility, self-trust, and quietude. It speaks to us in undertones, guiding us toward the right path aligned with our souls.'

The seekers scoffed at his words, accustomed to concrete volumes. Yet, those who heeded his advice and sought within themselves, discovered the answers they had been seeking.

Moral of the Parable: The intuition within us is the best guide to determining our life's path; all we need to do is listen.

Uninvited Advisory

Once upon a time, there was a diligent bee known for its productivity. It fashioned its hive in the heart of a large, robust tree. The bee tirelessly collected honey, seldom taking the chance to sit back and enjoy the fruits of its efforts.

One day, a caterpillar, sluggish and unhurried compared to the busy bee, approached the tree. Each day it observed the bee, gathering honey, endlessly engaged. Offended by the bee's constant toil, the caterpillar described the peace of a slow life, the pleasure of doing nothing. Yet, the bee continued, its buzz a perpetual companion to the forest.

As the caterpillar transformed into a butterfly and took to the skies, the bee finally collapsed, exhausted, its hive abundant with honey. The butterfly passed by the tree, its eyes filled with sympathy but its heart full of understanding. The bee not despairing its drop, but celebrating its fruitfulness. It finally understood, that counsel unsought, regardless of intention, may not be beneficial. For one's inner voice oftentimes knows better the course that should be pursued.

How the Wind Talks

A seasoned sailor set forth on an enormous journey across the ocean. This was no common adventure, it veered from his usual course, driving him towards uncharted horizons. Despite the unknown, the sailor was not fearful; he had prepared for the journey the best he could.

However, as he pushed against the water's resistance, he found the silent pressure of the winds. It spoke to him, but in ways he wasn't used to. There were no loud thunderous roars, no climatic ups and downs, only the quiet ripple of the vast ocean orchestrated by the guiding winds. The signs were subtle, the messages embedded in the gentle flow, but he was determined to understand.

Gradually, he adjusted, mustering patience even amidst the deafening silence. He stayed in the moment, observing, feeling... allowing his innate senses to interpret the whispers of the wind. And slowly, he found a rhythm, a harmony struck between him, his vessel, and the wind. The journey transformed into a commune, an interplay of energies that the sailor felt deep within his spirit.

Harmony in Silence

In an ancient forest lived a solitary monk renowned for his wisdom. However, he never spoke; his teachings were encapsuled in silence. Yet, individuals seeking enlightenment would trek through mountains to sit in his quiet presence.

One day, an impatient scholar, frustrated with the monk's silence, demanded, 'If you do not speak, how are we to learn anything?' Without uttering a word, the monk handed the scholar a seashell.

The scholar perceived silence from the shell initially. However, upon patience, he heard the echo of the distant ocean's waves, feeling the vibrations from a world unnoticed before. He realized, in that calming silence, one hears the unsaid, feeling the wisdom whispers that guide from within.

Unseen Signals

There was a hamlet, hidden amidst verdant hills, blessed with a peaceful ambience and friendly folk. The villagers believed every child born in their hamlet bore the touch of the celestial. As a symbol of this belief, they would plant a tree for each newborn, which they believed would grow in synchrony with the child.

Each person nurtured their tree, in the process understanding its needs intuitively. Seasonal changes, the softening of the soil, the aura of the tree – all guided one in this ritual. An old villager, the oldest living, had outlived the others. Saddened by his solitude, he would spend his time sitting underneath his old, sturdy tree. It served as his constant companion, reminding him of his bygone years.

One day, the villagers awoke to find the old man's tree fluttering with a peculiar rhythm. They rushed to the old man's hut only to find him living his last moments. The tree, it seemed, was transmitting the unseen signals of the old man's life-force. A silent communication, beyond words, understood only in emotions and silent vibrations - a song of the soul.

The Unsung Oracle

In a shimmering land far, far away, there lived a renowned oracle famed for her prophesies. Her words shaped the destiny of empires and monarchs. Yet, her most profoundly moving counsel wasn't in her words but the silence that followed. People often overlooked this second counsel, for it was not delivered in speeches or predictions, but in the peaceful quiet that ensued. Their minds buzzing with her words would miss the silent prophecy awaiting in her profound quietness. So, the unspoken wisdom of the oracle remained hidden, only known to those rare few who could let go of their anxieties, embracing the tranquil stillness.

The calm that followed her prophesies was just as essential as her forewarnings, reminding us that what is not said can be as impactful as what is said. Interpretations often differ, but the truth only understood by those who had learned to appreciate silence as an oracle of guidance in their lives, acknowledging the 'Unsung Oracle'.

Inner Mirror Reflects

In the royal palace of Banyan Kingdom, a valuable mirror was kept. Legend was that this mirror never lied. It was said that whoever looked into the mirror would not behold their physical form, but their very essence, their true nature.

The king had a wise advisor - an old sage who was known for his innate foresight. The king, intrigued by the mirror's legend, called the sage for assistance. When asked about the mirror, the sage explained, 'The mirror simply suggests what's within. It is devoid of distortion, reflecting only truth.'

The king then questioned why he often saw himself contradictory in the mirror. The sage kindly replied, 'In your heart, you know what is true. The mirror merely reflects the pure interior, in no way can it lie. It's your perception that's clouded.' Recognizing the wisdom of his advisor, the king learned the importance of acknowledging and honoring his internal impulses before seeking validation from external entities.

Invisible Hands Guiding

Once, in a small village isolated by towering mountains, lived a blind potter named Bertok. His talent was unparalleled, despite never observing his own creations. He claimed that invisible hands guided him, dictating the shape, the curve, the form of every pot he produced.

Skeptic villagers shrugged it off as a trick, some claimed that he was deceiving everyone. One day, the village leader threw a challenge at Bertok. 'Produce a pot which carries the essence of our village and I shall believe you,' he declared. Bertok, unfazed, accepted the challenge.

In the dead of the night, he sat at his potter's wheel. To the casual observer, it seemed Bertok was blindly throwing clay around, but Bertok felt a direction, a push. Guided by the invisible hands, he went through a medley of emotions. He felt the heartbeat of the village, its joys, despair, triumphs, and defeats.

What took shape was a masterpiece that left the village leader in awe. It rightfully portrayed the spirit of the village, capturing its essence uncannily. That day, the village understood — Bertok's magic was real. These were not mere invisible hands, but unseen forces within him, guiding those graceful creations.

Riddle of the Inner Guide

A skeptical scholar named Finnagon arrived in Mylonia, intrigued by tales of an oracle who gave cryptic yet accurate advice. Skeptical, Finnagon proposed a challenge. He presented to the oracle a sealed scroll, whose contents were known to him alone, and asked the oracle to reveal its contents.

'I do not see through sealed scrolls or hidden intentions,' replied the Oracle, 'but feel what is needed by the heart that seeks.' Disappointed, Finnagon turned to leave but stopped as the Oracle spoke again. 'Your scroll contains a map, does it not?' Finnagon asked how he knew. The Oracle replied, 'Your heart seeks knowledge and purpose, much like a traveler with a map.'

Stunned, Finnagon understood. It was not about reading scrolls or minds, but listening to the echoes of the heart. He had not simply revealed an object, but understood the intention behind it. It was not divination but resonating with the nuances of human desires.

Inner Waves of Understanding

An experienced sailor, old Osmund, was renowned throughout his seaside town for his unrivaled ability to predict stormy weather, even when the sea was calm and the sun was shining. The secret to this, he said, lay in his careful observation of the subtle upswelling of the waves.

Over time, many asked Osmund to teach his technique. So Osmund gathered interested folks and guided them through understanding the tidings of the ocean. They observed, listened, and focused on the ocean. Yet, none could grasp the concept except for young Bael, who successfully started predicting the storms.

People questioned: 'How could young Bael understand the waves while the others failed?' Bael disclosed that he paid close attention not just to the ocean's waves but also to the feelings inside him, mirroring the sea's rhythm. By correlating the two, Bael explained, he could anticipate the ocean's mood. The others had only been observing the ocean, while young Bael listened to his inner waves.

The Unvoiced Prophesy

Savara was a gifted but mute seer of Metropolis, known to predict world events in her mysterious code. The mayor, intrigued by her reputation, approached Savara to help his city avert possible calamities. As Savara presented her next prophecy in her unspoken language, the mayor found himself unable to understand. He tried decoding gestures, mimics, the intensity of her eye contact, but all in vain.

A month later, a sudden famine hit Metropolis. The mayor, repenting he couldn't understand Savara's message, approached her again. She repeated her unspoken prophecy which he still couldn't decrypt. Even so, rather than just observing, he started feeling the emotions Savara was projecting. He felt an urge to store food and water, to shelter the homeless. Without understanding why, he acted on his feelings, which ultimately helped the city overcome worst times.

Later realizing that Savara's prophecy was extracted through an emotional connection, the mayor accepted that Savara's unvoiced messages were not meant to fall onto the ears but resonate within the soul, realizing that the voiceless prophecy was provided as an intuition-guided action, not to be translated in words but felt within. He had understood the language of emotions, the unvoiced prophesy.

Eternal Compass: The Guide

There was once a seasoned mariner named Leif who embarked on extensive voyages across unknown seas. But he never got lost, all thanks to his golden compass passed down the generations. It wasn't just any compass, but one that didn't point North, instead it always directed towards his home.

On one journey, amidst a fierce storm, the golden compass was swept away. Leif was left distraught and feared he could never find his way home. But soon, the sea calmed, and Leif felt an inexplicable instinct guiding him. He followed it, and journeyed successfully back home.

Then onwards, Leif learned to trust his internal compass, his instinct, which guided him aptly just as his golden compass did. It became his trusted guide, his eternal compass that led him through every storm.

Unconscious Whispers

In a remote village nestled between the tallest mountains and the deepest forests, there lived a simple baker. He was known throughout the land for his sumptuous bread, flawlessly kneaded and remarkably golden. One fateful day, his trusted oven betrayed him, engulfing his bakery in a rage of flames. The baker was left with nothing.

With no bread to sell, no oven to bake, he sat by the ashes, contemplating his misfortune when he realized he could hear the faint murmurs of the fire in his dreams. They didn't guide him, didn't offer instructions, but they echoed in his unconscious. Being a man of pragmatism, the baker chose to dismiss them.

However, the fire's whispers became louder each night, too prominent to ignore. One morning, the baker took a leap into the unknown. He began rebuilding his bakery, not according to practical expectations, but following the soft murmurs he heard in his dreams. Many accused him of madness while others pitied his lost pragmatism.

Yet, when the new ovens fired up, the resurgence of the tantalizing aroma of fresh bread proved them wrong. The bakery now attracted people from every corner of the kingdom. The simple baker had created the unlikeliest marvel, guided by the whispers from the shadows of his dreams.

Unvoiced Dialogues of the Soul

In the heart of a bustling city lived a tailor named Aditya regarded for his unmatched craftsmanship. Among his patrons was a quiet nobleman who seldom expressed much but often visited Aditya.

Every few weeks, the nobleman would bring a silken fabric and ask Aditya to make a robe. While working on the robes, Aditya attempted to understand the nobleman's mood. The quiet nobleman's fabrics were his silent languages, and the colours echoed with the unvoiced dialogues of his soul. The vibrant colours mirrored jovial energy, while the subdued shades hinted at quiet introspection.

Aditya learned to listen to these silent articulations.
It made him realize the depth of silent speak and the powerful resonance of what isn't explicitly voiced but rather felt at the core.

The Inward Mentor

As an orphaned child, a farmer had to rely on his instincts for survival. His will to live was strong, and by working diligently and cautiously, he slowly made a humble life for himself. As he became comfortable, he began to ignore his inward mentor, the voice that guided him through his youth. He thought himself wise enough to face adversities alone.

One day, he decided to plant a new seed, a mysterious lookalike of the famous Golden Apple tree. Days turned to months, and the vibrant tree sprouted apples that glowed with exquisite golden hues, much to the farmer's delight. Enchanted by the prospects of wealth and prosperity, the farmer busied himself with the harvest. A faint voice from within cautioned him, but he brushed it off.

To his disappointment, what appeared to be golden apples were lifeless illusions – crumpling to dust as soon as they were touched. Devastated, he reflected on his actions and realized he had not heeded his inward mentor. From that day forward, he pledged to always absorb the wisdom his internal guide offered.

The Guide in the Shadows

In the heart of a thriving city, lived a prosperous merchant. Known for his keen eye for priceless artifacts, he invested his wealth in treasures from distant lands. Among his most priceless possessions, was an uncanny shadow box, whose importance he hadn't realized.

One time, the merchant found himself drawn towards a beguiling statue in an auction. Everything about this artifact screamed danger, yet its allure was overpowering. He saw the overwhelming bids as a sign of prestige and contemplated to invest his fortune. That night, rest eluded him as he kept thinking about the statue.

Unable to sleep, he spent the night mulling over his impending decision by the shadow box. As he stared at the box, the shadows danced and shifted, forming a clear image of the statue breaking and leaving destruction in its wake. Intrigued, he took the warning to heart and rescinded his desire to purchase the statue.

Within days, news spread about the buyer who had won the statue, meeting an unfortunate end as the artifact shattered into a thousand pieces, destroying all wealth in its vicinity. The merchant, realizing the significance of the shadow box, thanked his hidden guide for its foresight.

Unseen Navigator

In a coastal village, navigation was a skill essential to its people. All seafarers passed on the lore of the Unseen Navigator to their apprentices during their maiden voyage.

On one such voyage with novice seamen, Captain Nereus asked the apprentices to helm the ship through the open seas. Despite the maps, the compasses, and careful guidance, each apprentice struggled to steer the ship accurately.

Watching them grapple, the Captain asked, 'Why do you not seek help from the Unseen Navigator?' The apprentices looked confused; they had no inkling about this unseen entity.

Nereus, with a smile, asked them to close their eyes and listen to the symphony of the sea, the rhythm of their ship cutting through the water, and the whispers of the wind against the sails.

'Feel the sea, become one with our vessel, let the Unseen Navigator guide you.' Slowly they began to feel their anxieties recede, experiencing a palpable connection with the sea and the ship, an immediate knowing on how to steer.

The Unseen Navigator was their intuition, an unseen force that allowed them to understand their environment in a way maps and compasses could never reveal.

Hidden Beats within the Heart

In a distant land, there was a sculptor named Fabrizio. His hands sculpted such lifelike statues that many believed they carried an essence of life. His secret lay in a magical crystal that could capture the rhythm of a human heart.

The crystal would capture the unique rhythm of the heart, and Fabrizio would sculpt his statues in harmony with it. One day, the crystal slipped off Fabrizio's hands and shattered. All seemed lost until he started feeling strange irregular beats within his own heart.

He began to interpret those pulsations. They guided his hands crafting stunning sculptures. Fabrizio realised the magical crystal was not the source, but a medium to connect with the rhythm deep within his heart. He learned to chisel in tune with these hidden beats, thus revealing their latent divine potential.

The Inner Echo

Nestled amidst the harmony of the forest lived an elderly sage named Yael. Villagers came from afar to seek his wisdom, a wisdom he attributed to 'The Inner Echo'

Intrigued by Yael's wisdom, a curious scholar traveled to discover the source of 'The Inner Echo'. Upon reaching Yael's humble abode, he asked, 'Master, tell me about the Inner Echo. What conundrum is this that empowers you with such profound wisdom?'

Yael pointed at the forest around them and said, 'Find the tallest tree you can see, shout out a question and come back to me with the answer you hear.' The scholar did as he was instructed. Being gregarious with his wisdom, Yael knew that experiencing will teach the scholar more than any explanation.

The scholar was skeptical but intrigued. He shouted, 'What is the meaning of life?' His own voice echoed back. When he returned, Yael asked, 'What did you hear?' He shrugged, 'Nothing, but my own voice!'

Yael asked, 'How did you feel?' 'I didn't understand any meaning, but I felt an inexplicable comfort.' Yael nodded. 'That's your Inner Echo, you'll find even the toughest answers in its resonance. It's not about the echo you hear, but the echo you feel.'

The scholar left with the revelation that this 'Inner Echo' was his intuition. The wisdom Yael possessed came not from external sources but from within his own being, from listening to his Inner Echo.

CPSIA information can be obtained
at www.ICGtesting.com
Printed in the USA
LVHW051044210723
752977LV00005B/52